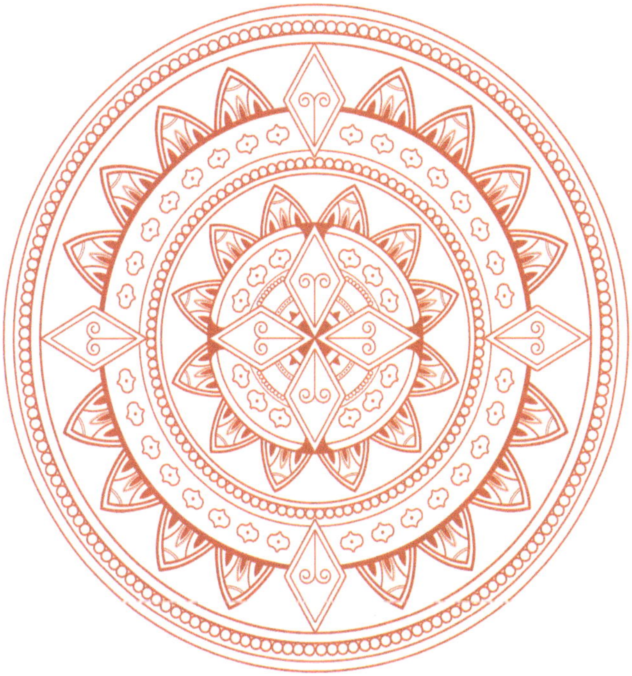

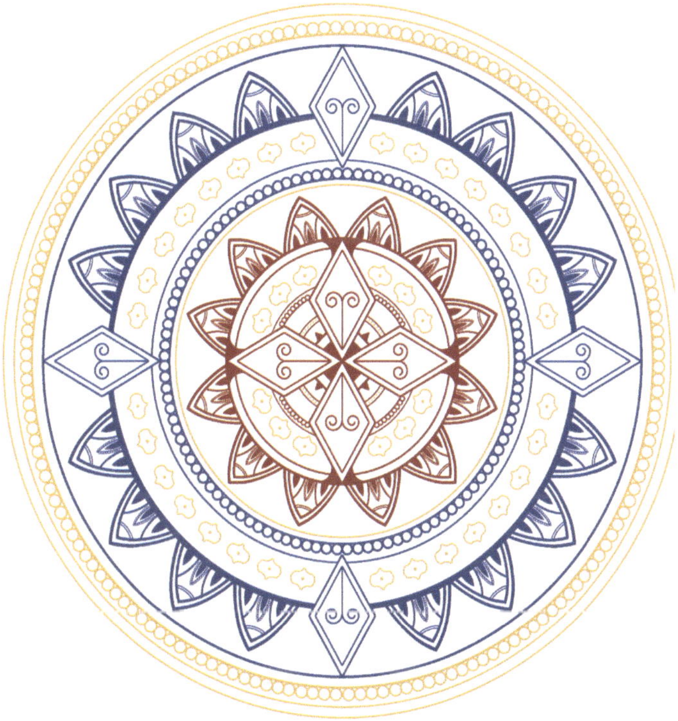

OPEN TO THE WORLD OF COLORS
MANDALAS

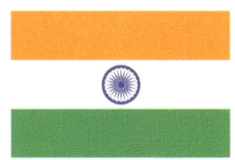

Instructions for use

Before coloring
Breathe, exhale and inhale.
Keep your hand upright.
Dream and Rehearse.

About the author: Filmmaker, passionate about colors, sensations and drawings.

DRAWINGS TO COLOR

Creating is Living!

GREGORI FIORINI

DRAWINGS TO COLOR
Creating is Living!

5

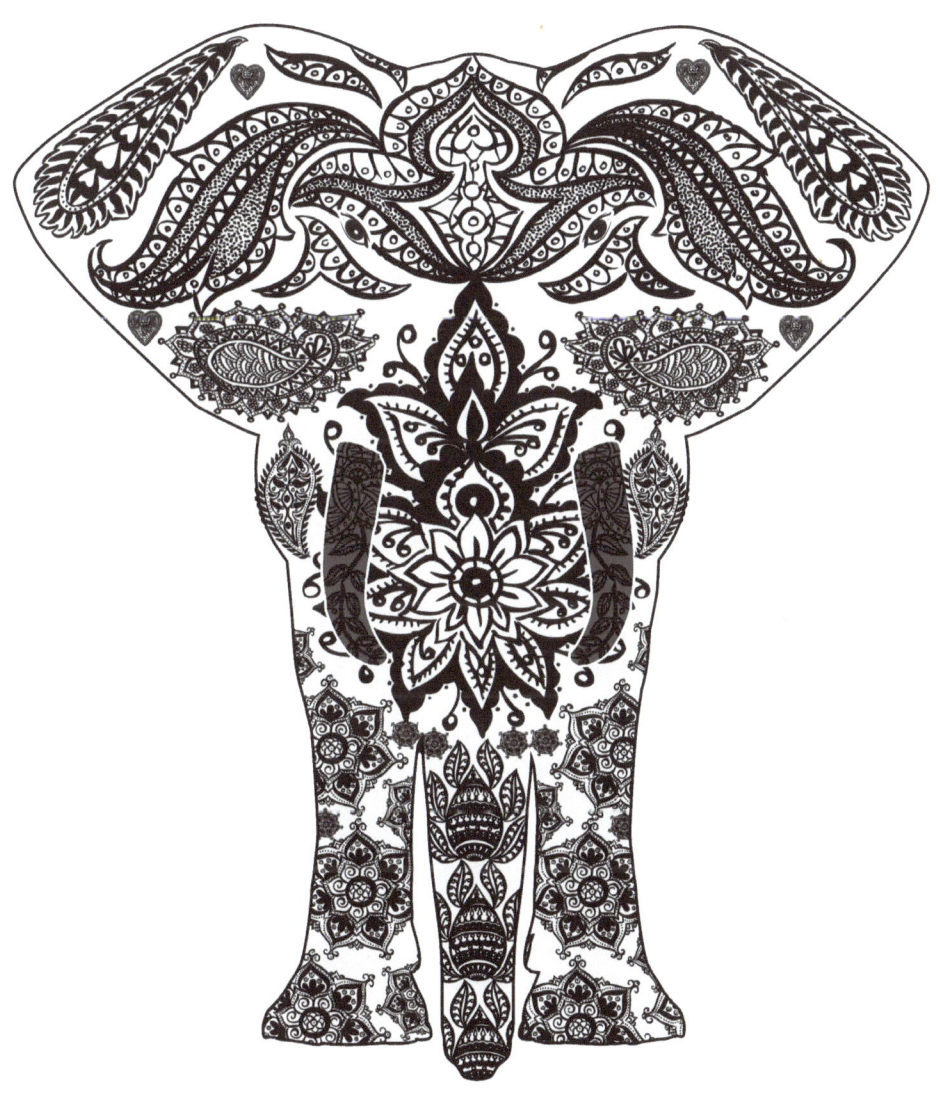

Difficulty level: MEDIUM

6

DRAWINGS TO COLOR
Creating is Living!

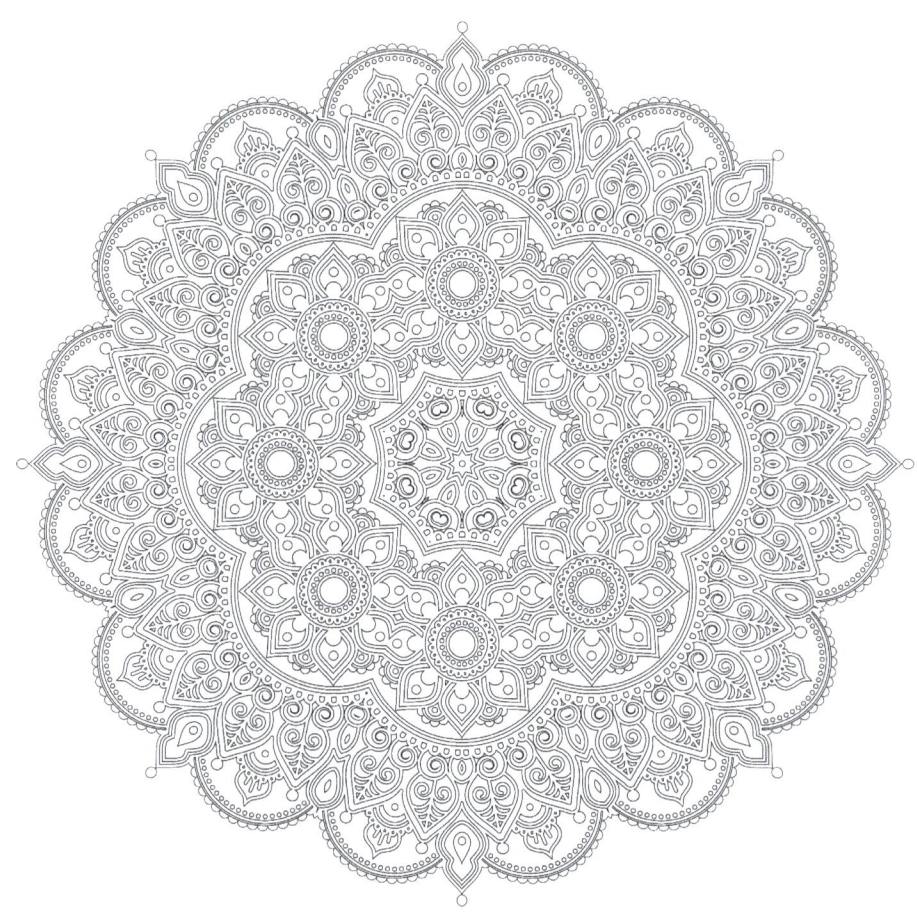

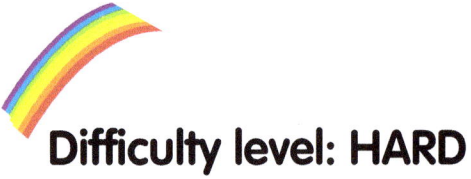
Difficulty level: HARD

DRAWINGS TO COLOR
Creating is Living!

7

🌈
Difficulty level: EASY

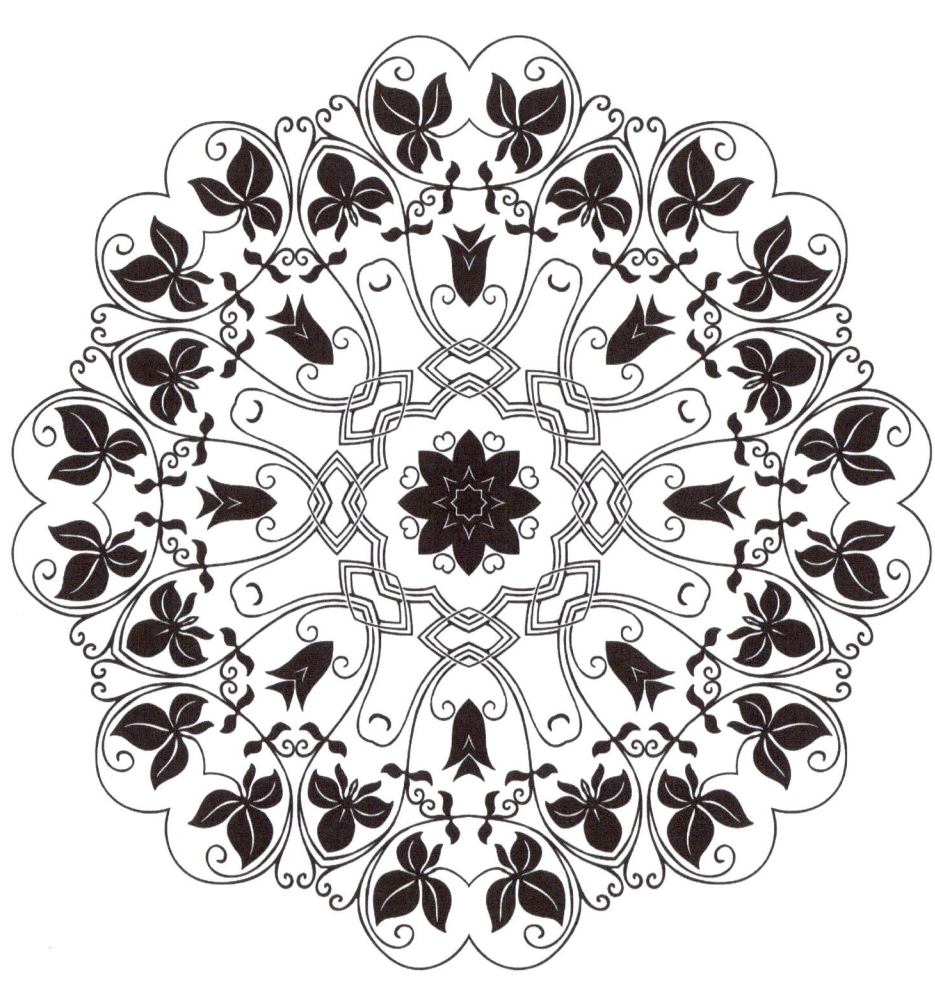

DRAWINGS TO COLOR
Creating is Living!

9

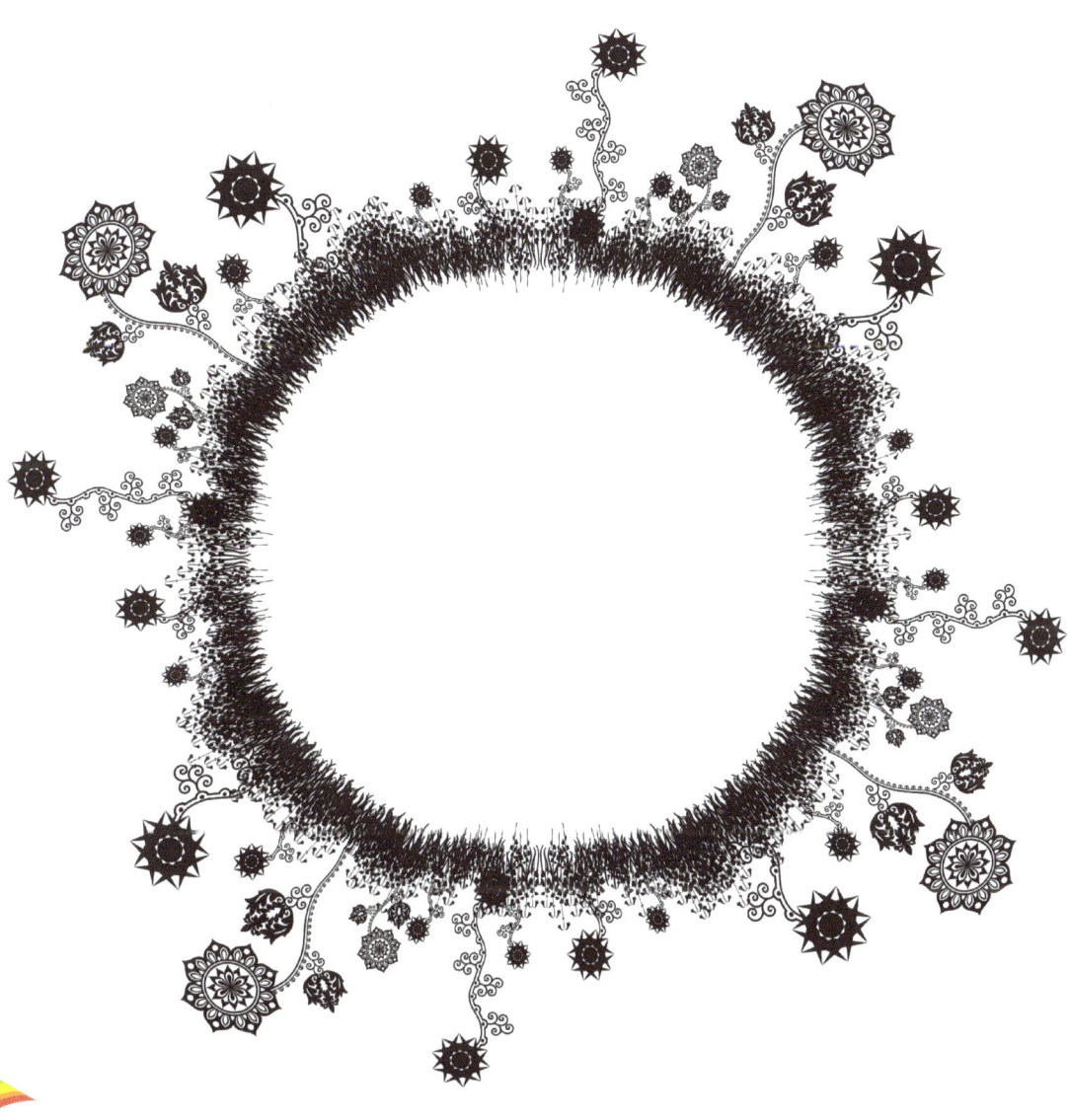

Difficulty level: HARD

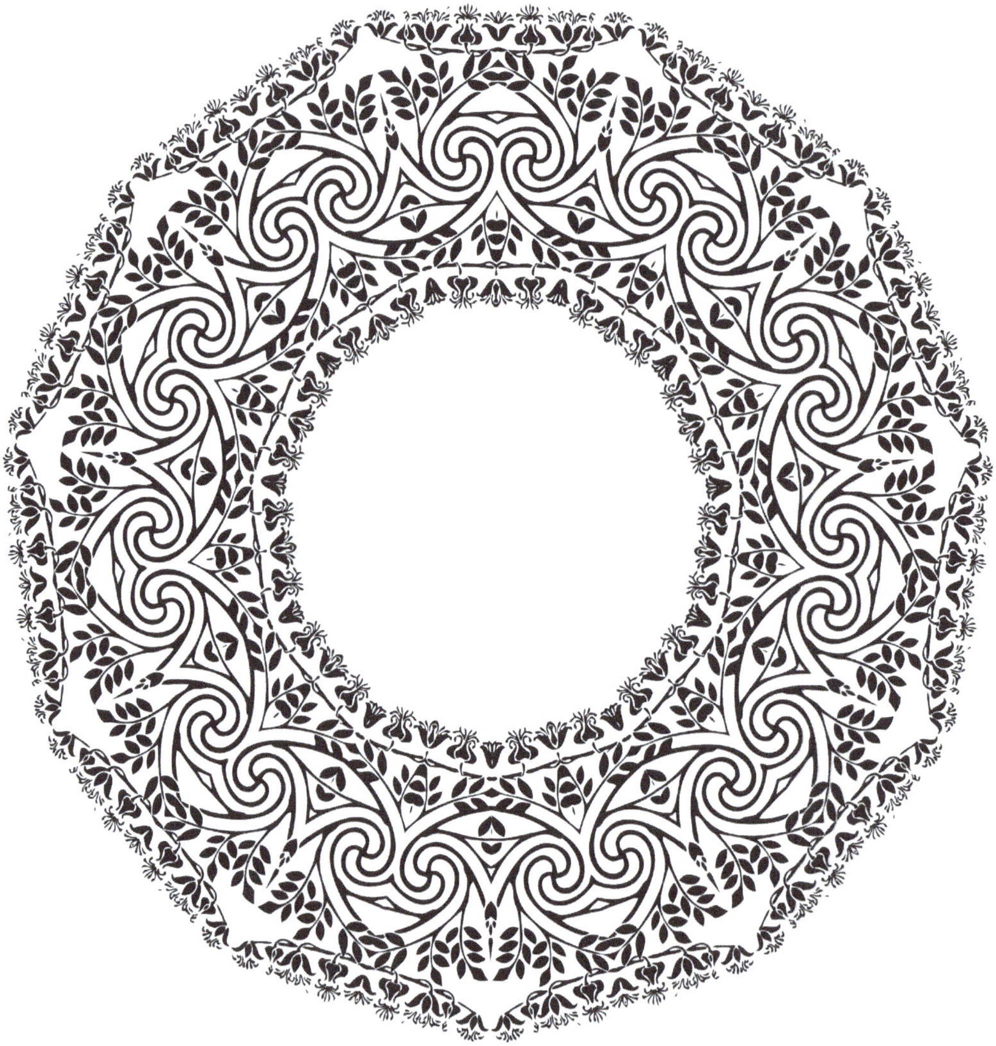

10

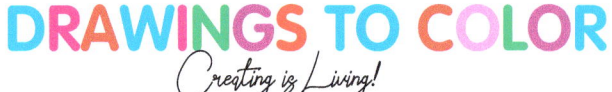

Difficulty level: MEDIUM

DRAWINGS TO COLOR
Creating is Living!

11

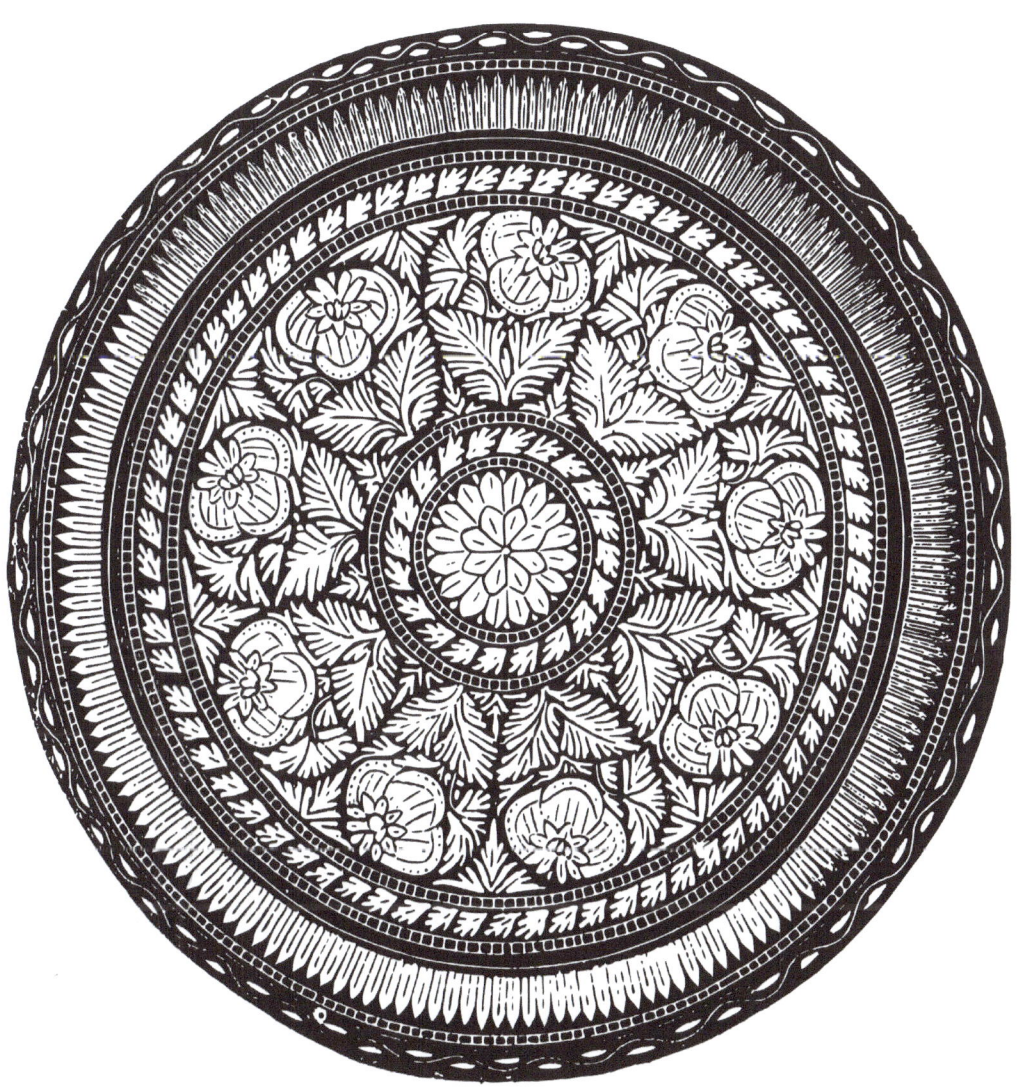

Difficulty level: HARD

12

DRAWINGS TO COLOR
Creating is Living!

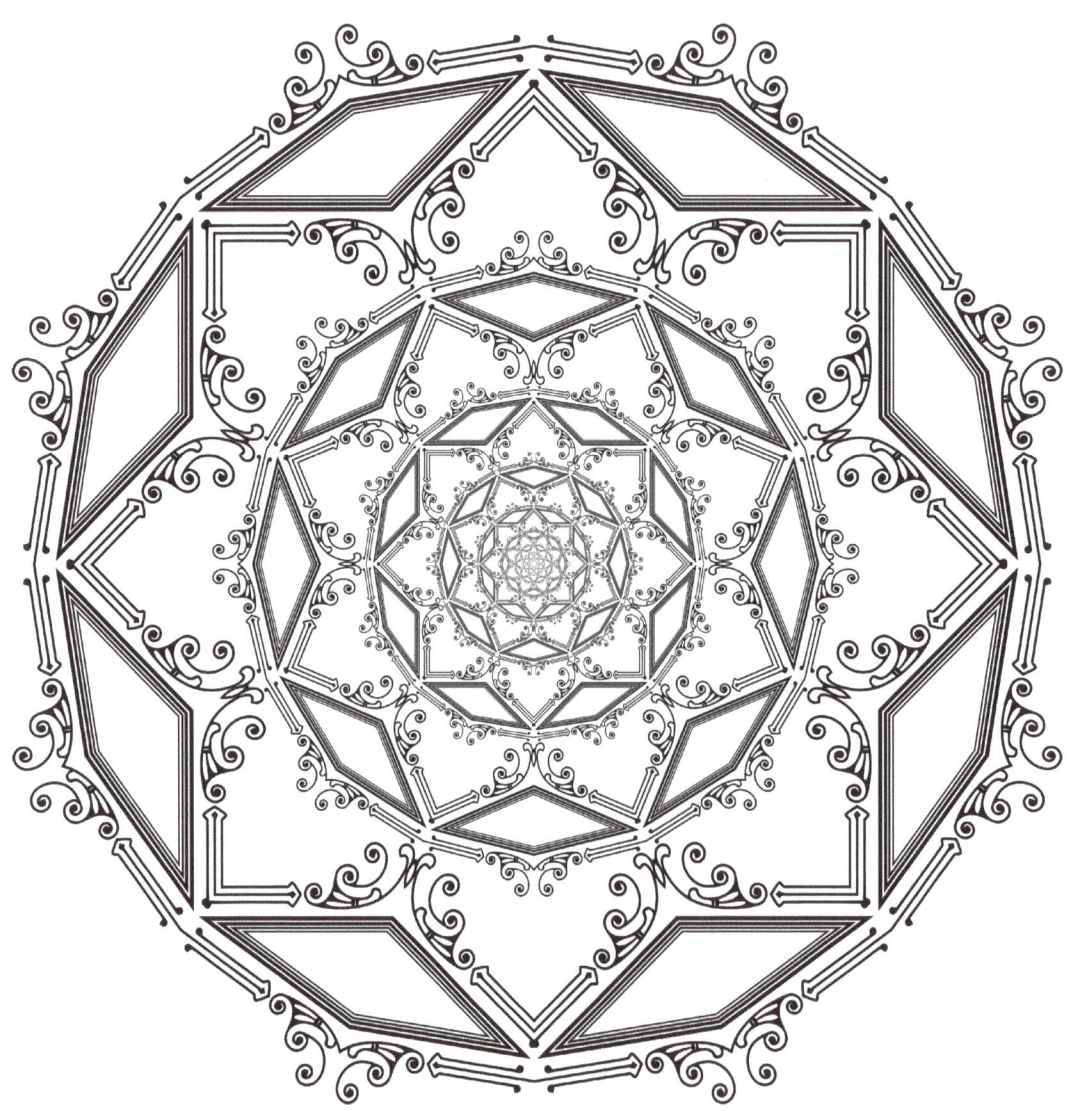

Difficulty level: MEDIUM

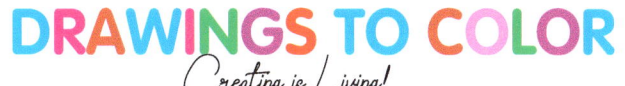

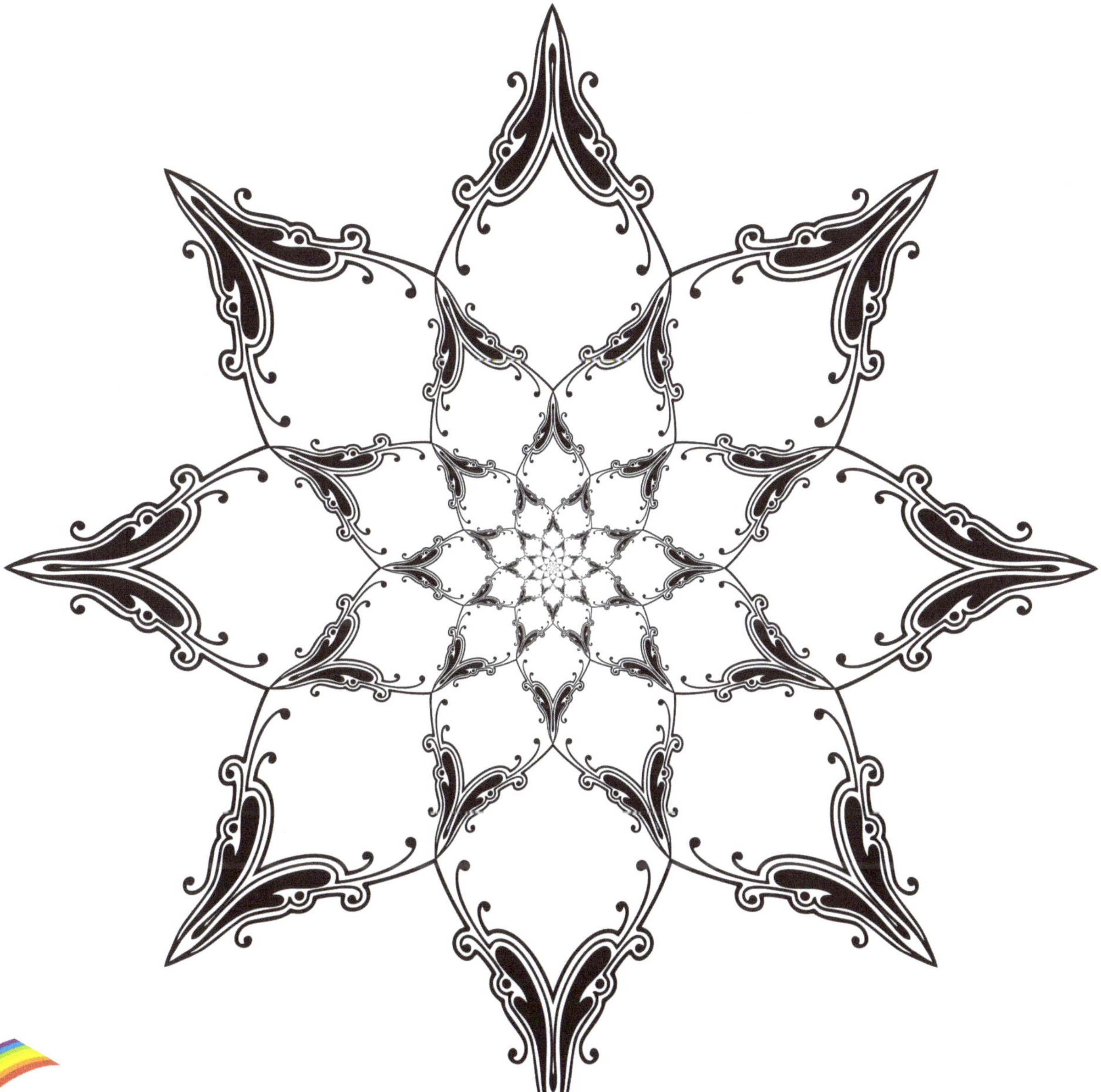

13

Difficulty level: EASY

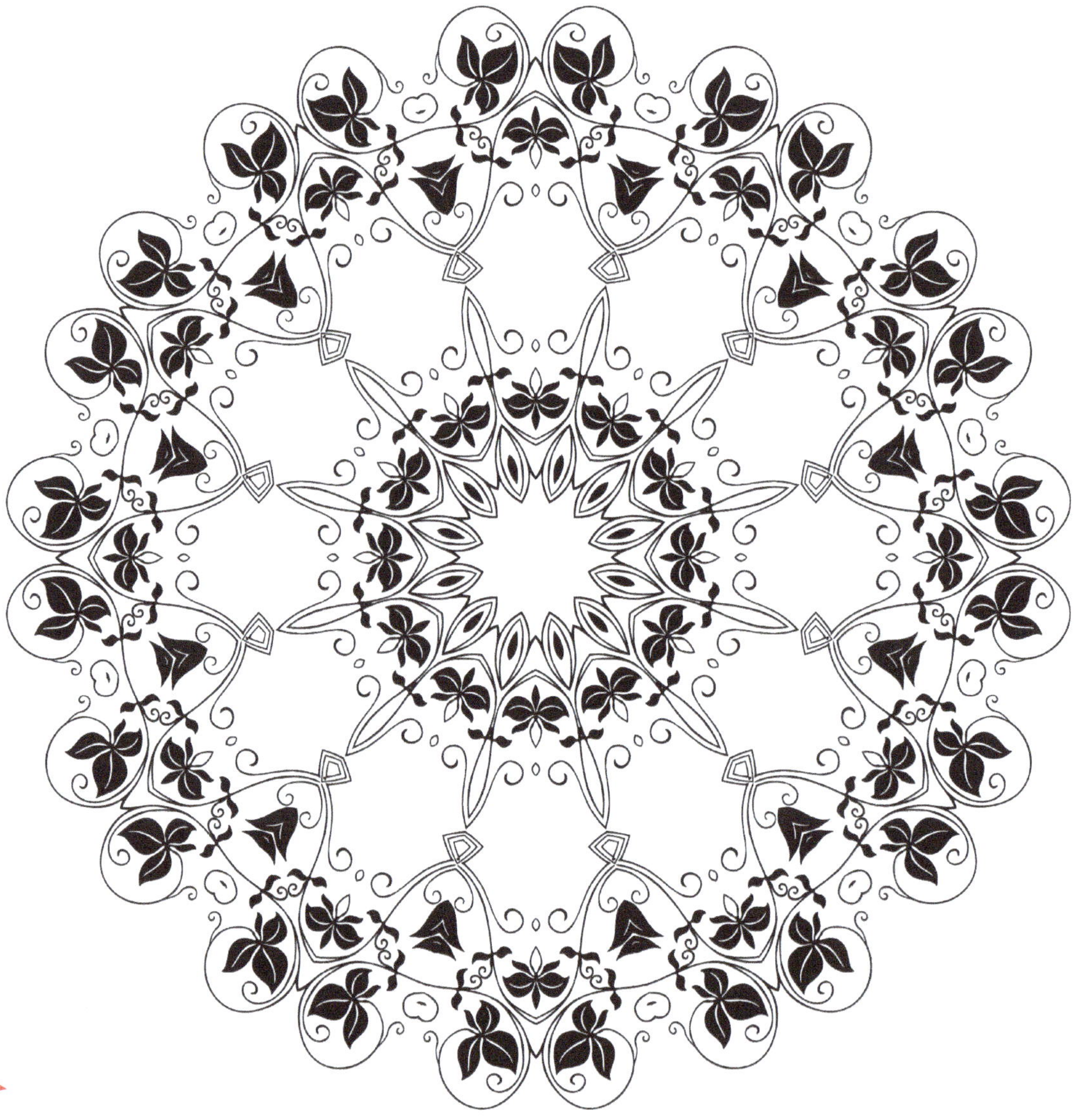

14

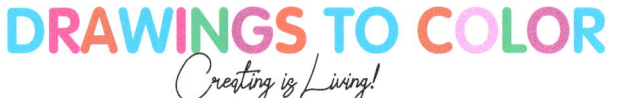

Difficulty level: MEDIUM

DRAWINGS TO COLOR
Creating is Living!

15

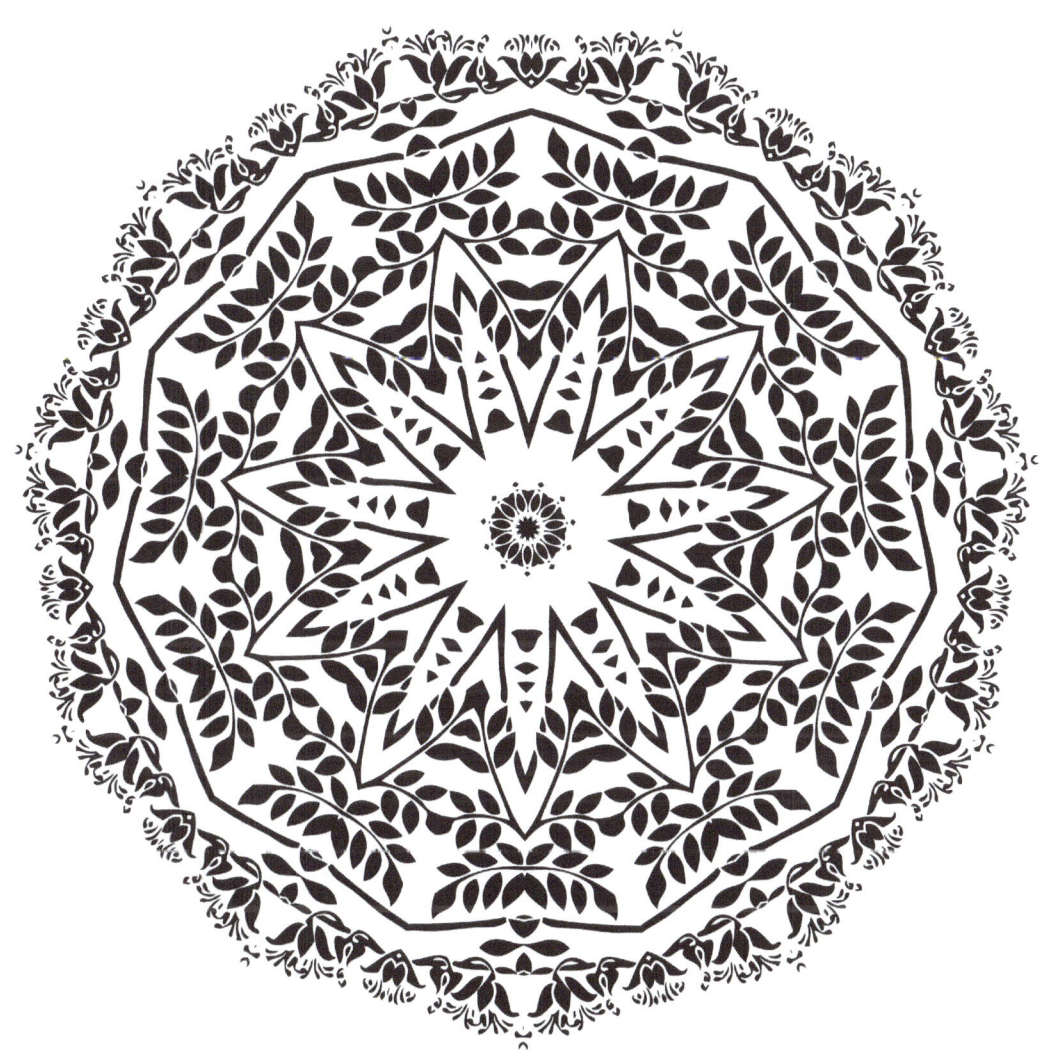

Difficulty level: MEDIUM

16 DRAWINGS TO COLOR
Creating is Living!

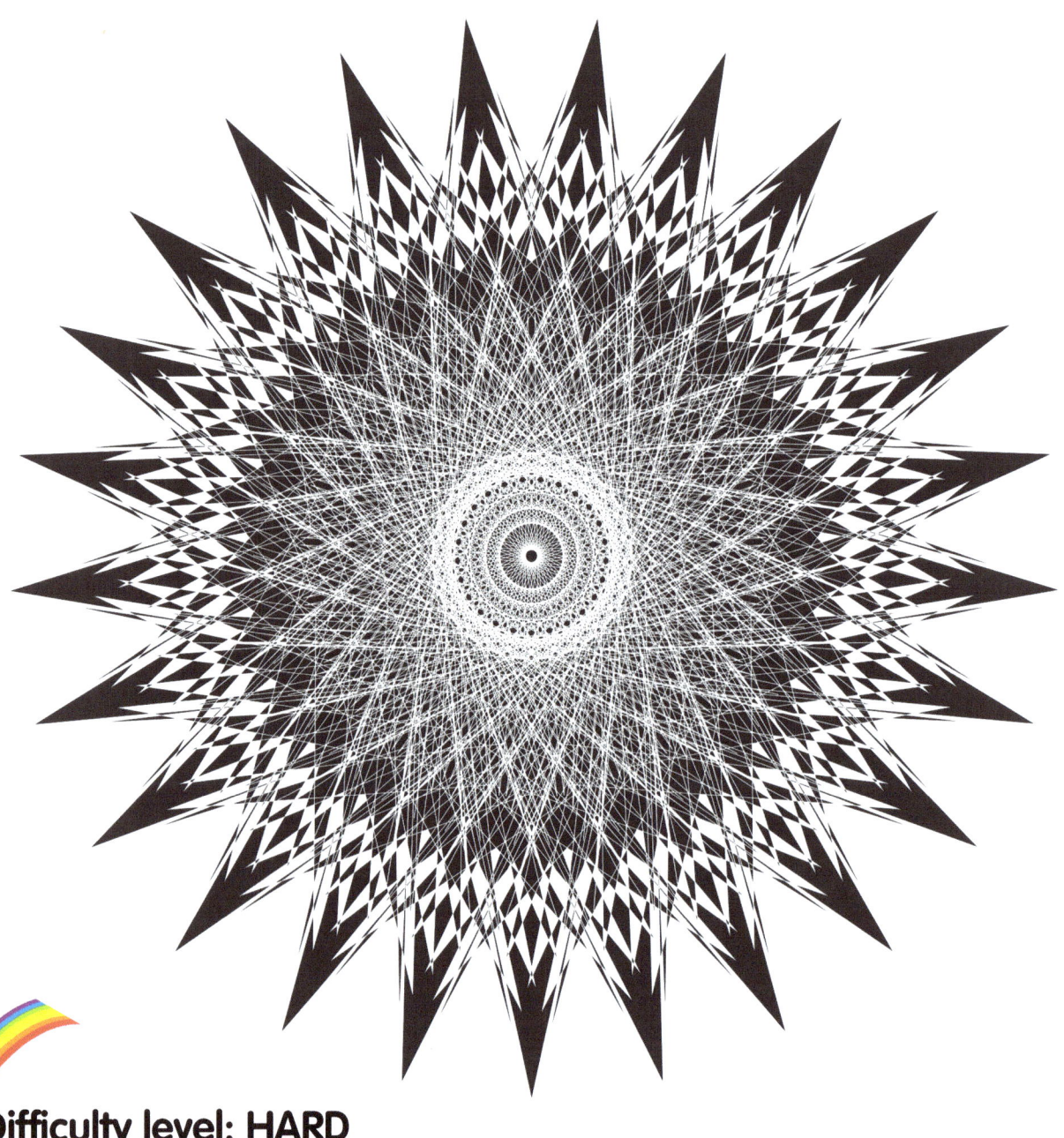

Difficulty level: HARD

DRAWINGS TO COLOR
Creating is Living!

17

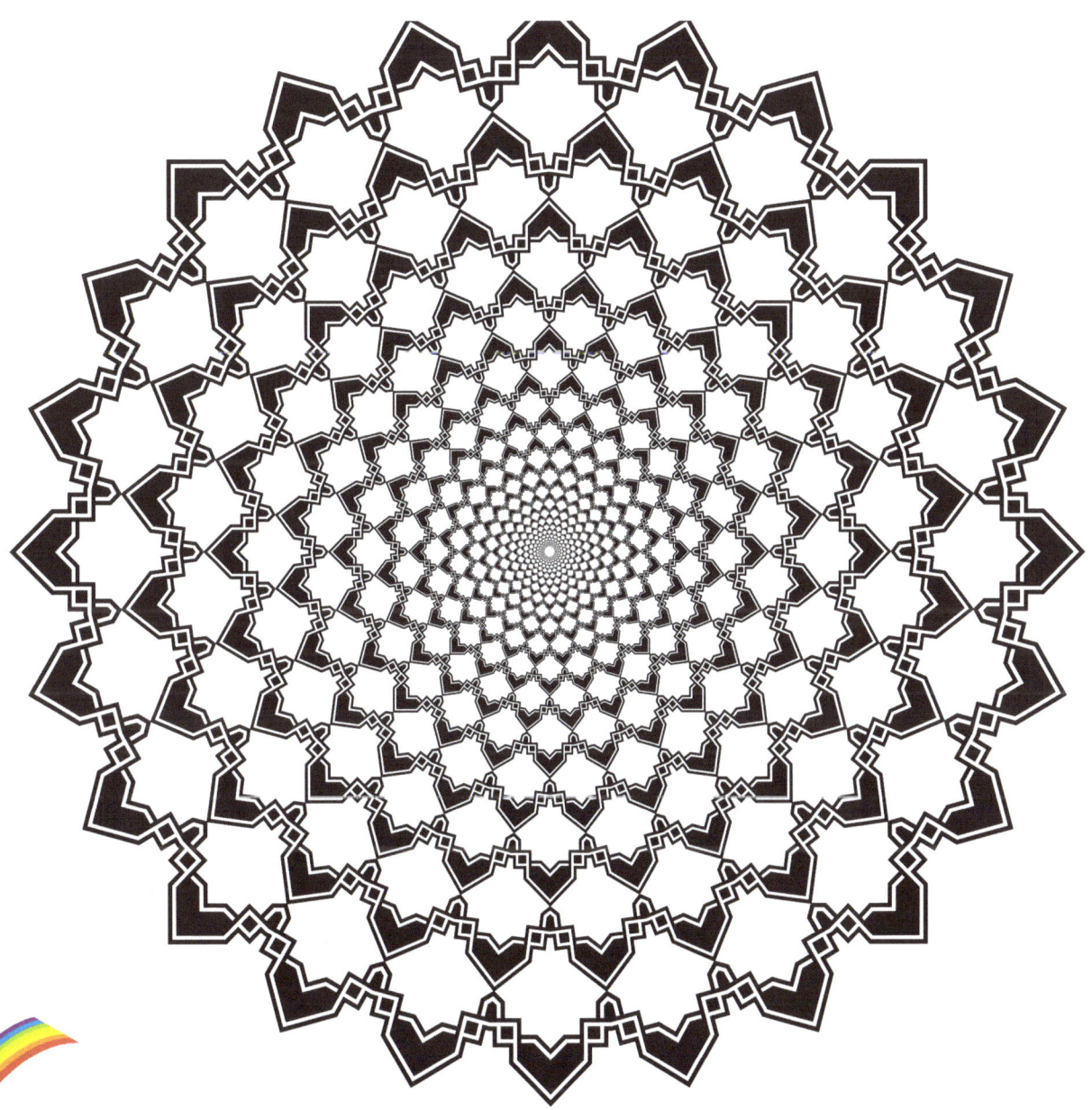

🌈 **Difficulty level: HARD**

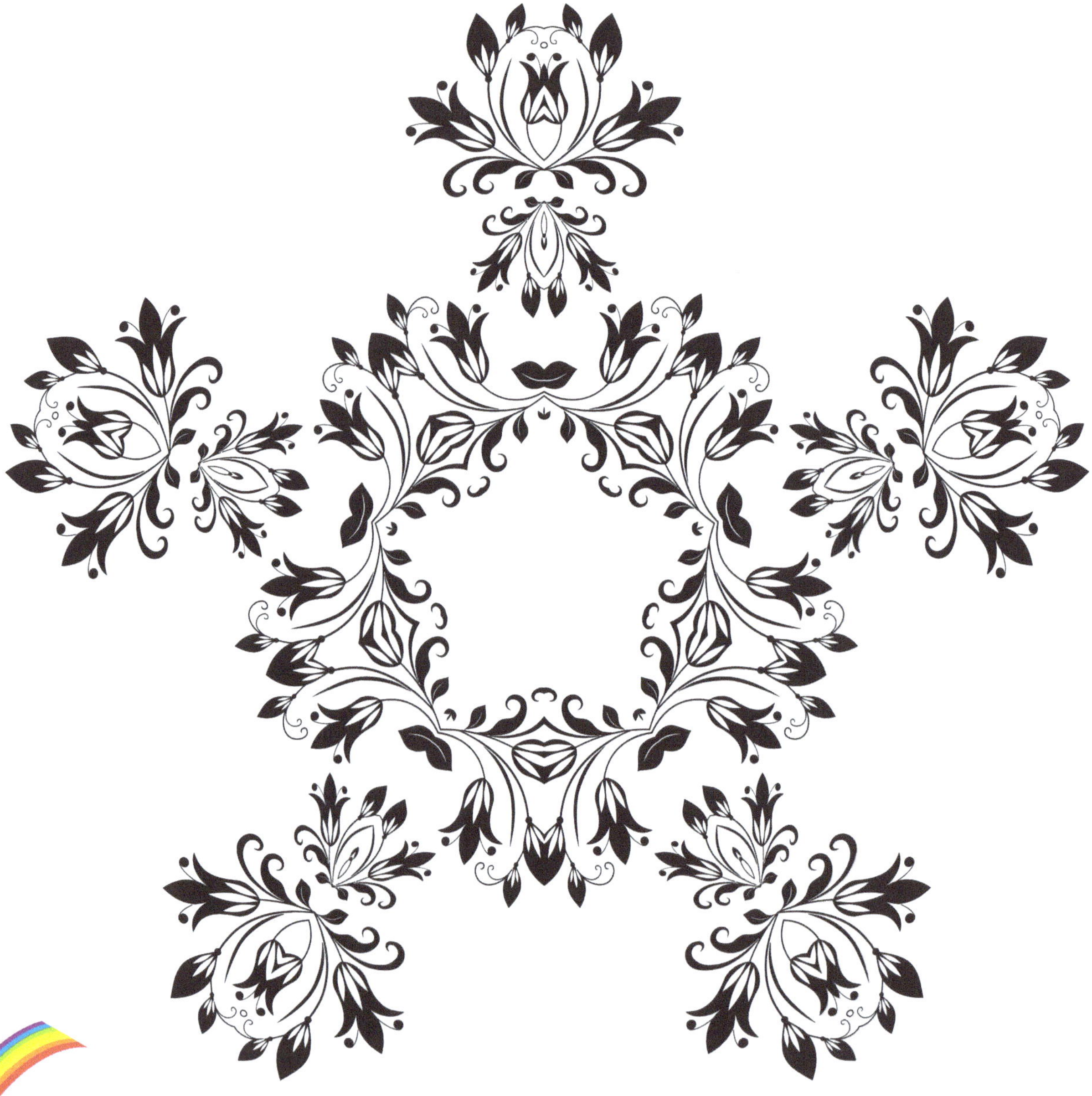

18

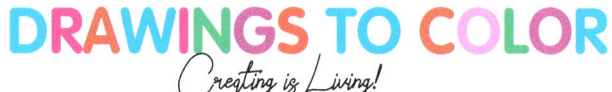

Difficulty level: EASY

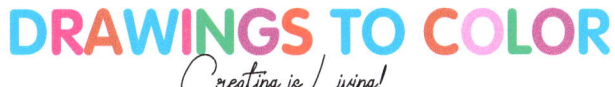

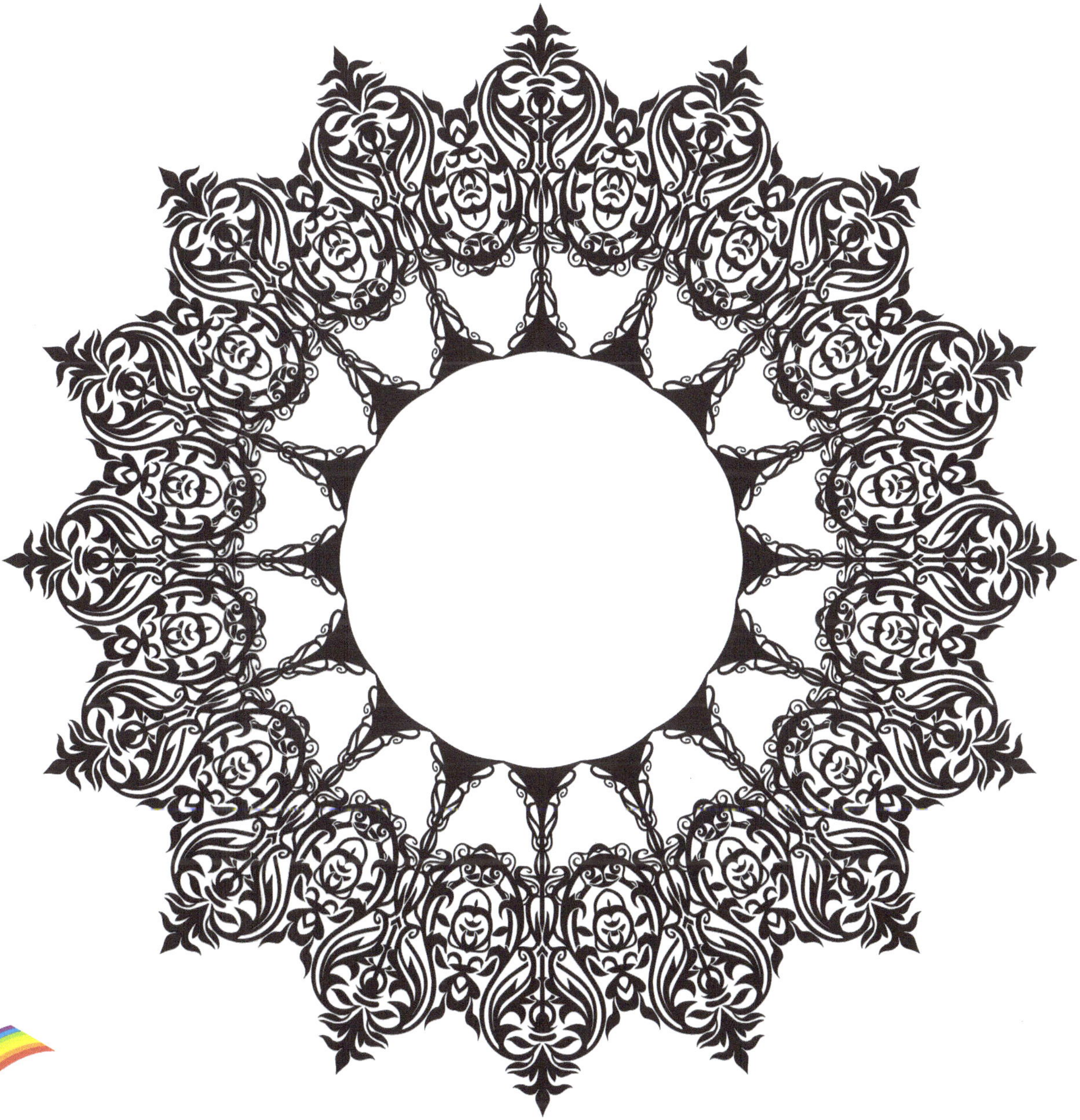

Difficulty level: MEDIUM

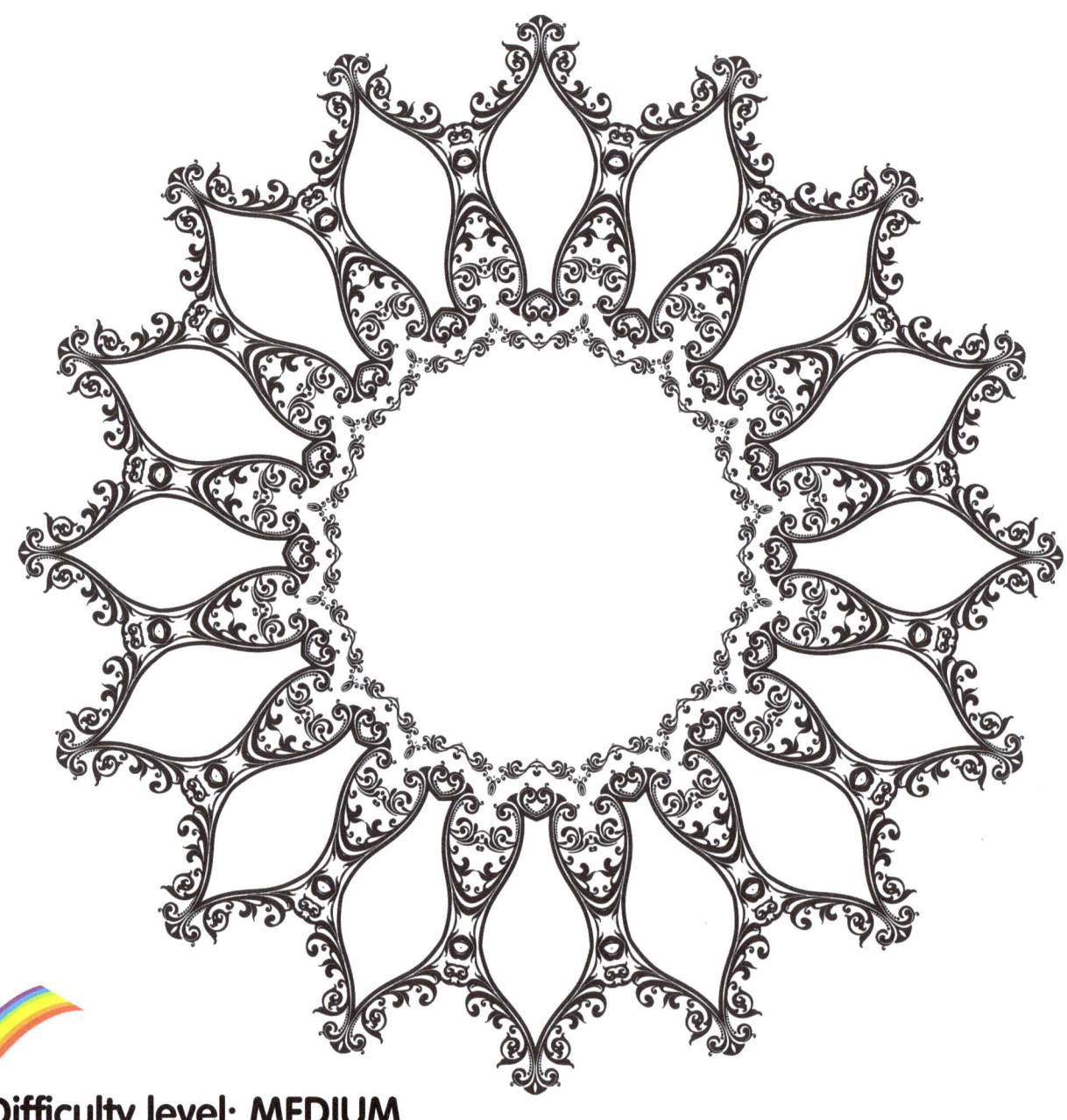

DRAWINGS TO COLOR
Creating is Living!

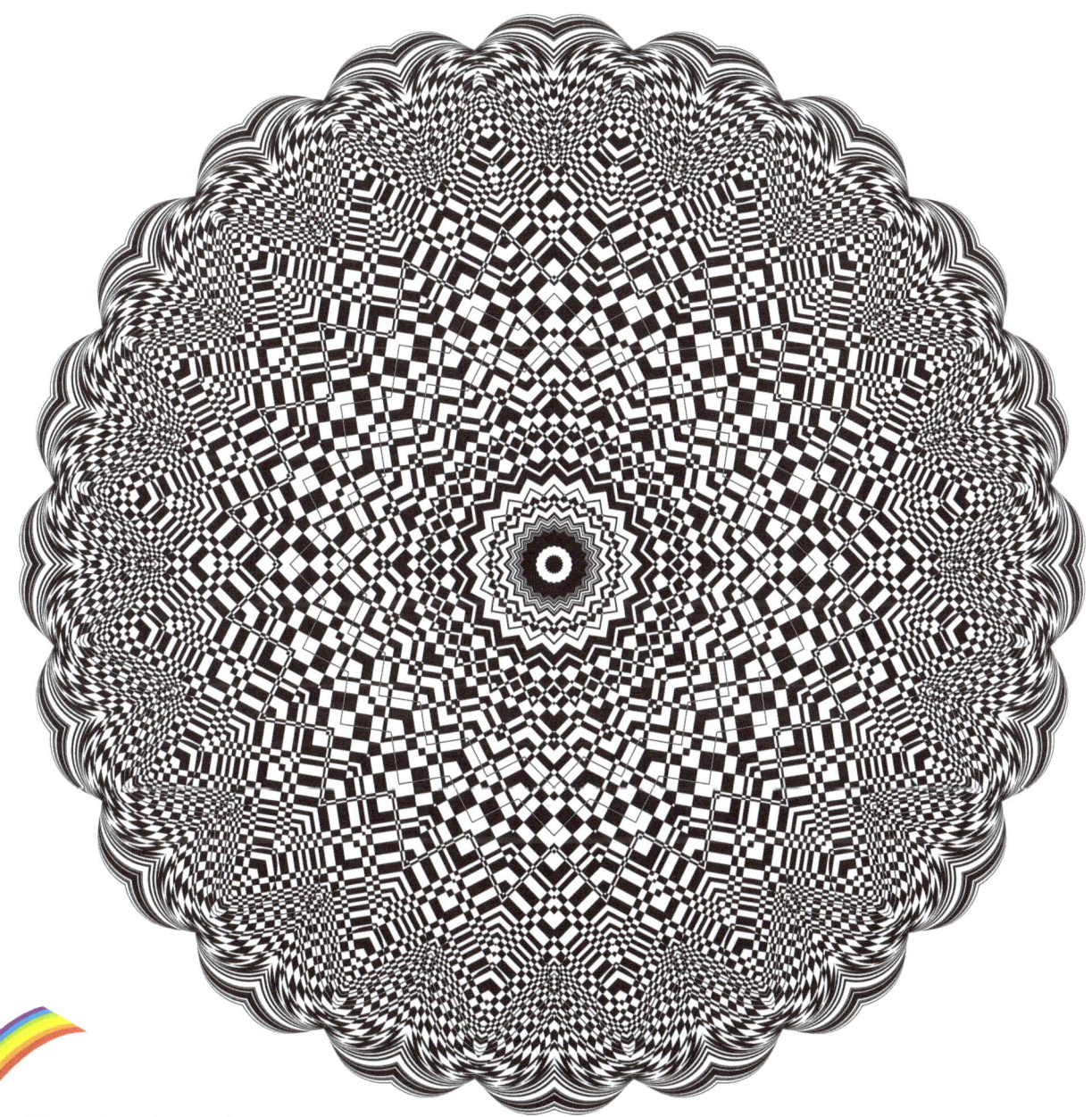

Difficulty level: HARD

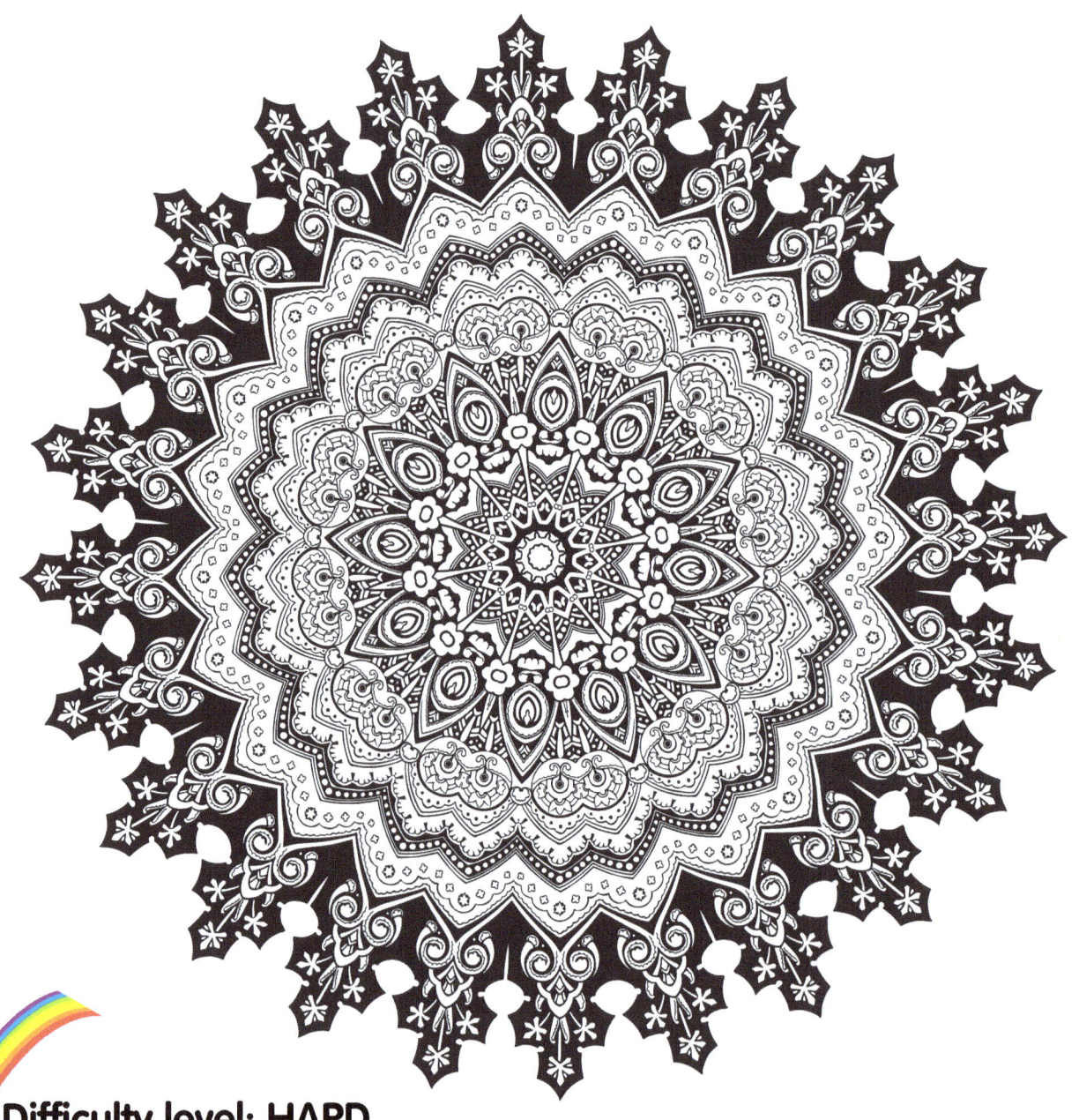

DRAWINGS TO COLOR
Creating is Living!

23

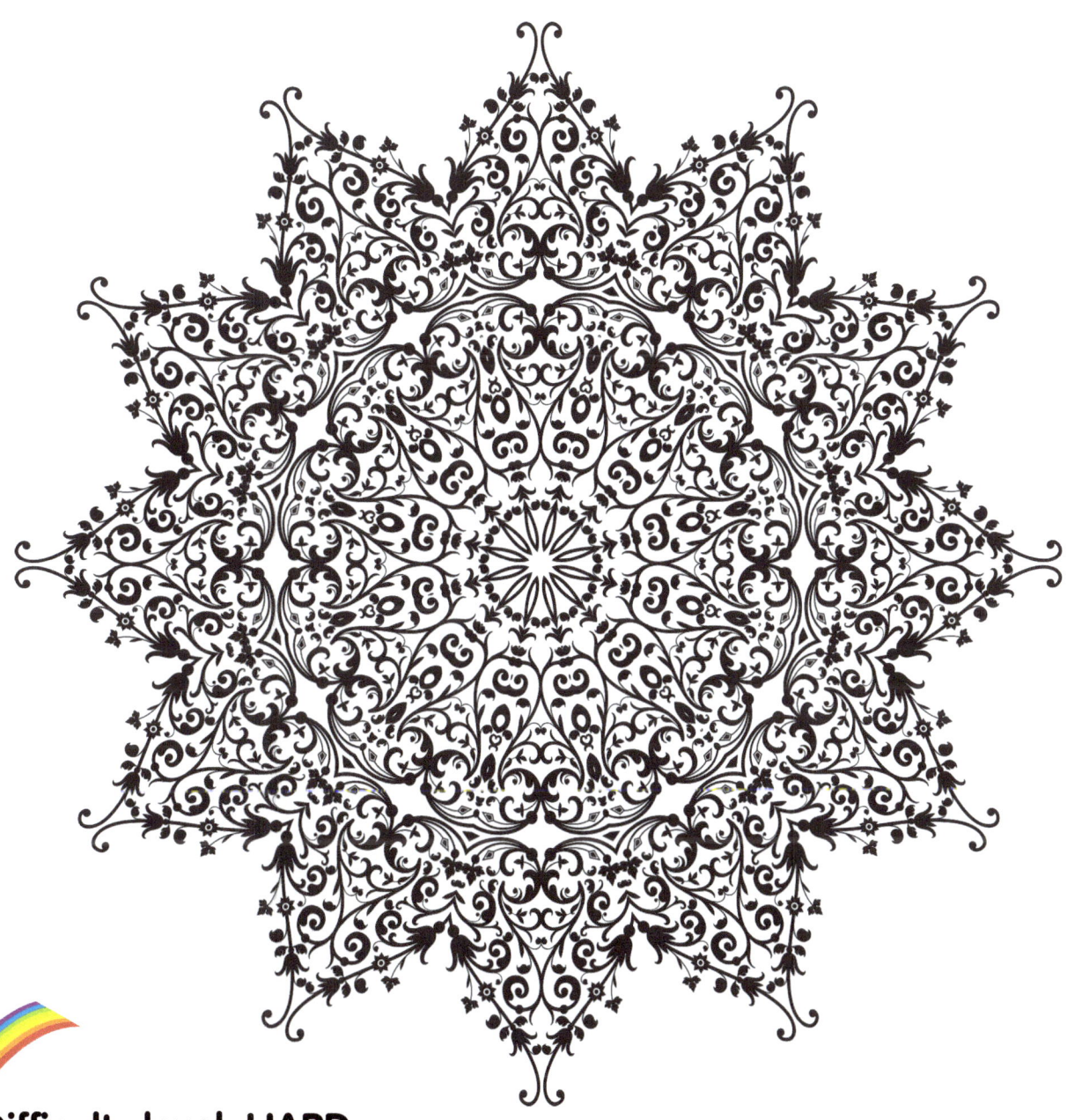

Difficulty level: HARD

24

DRAWINGS TO COLOR
Creating is Living!

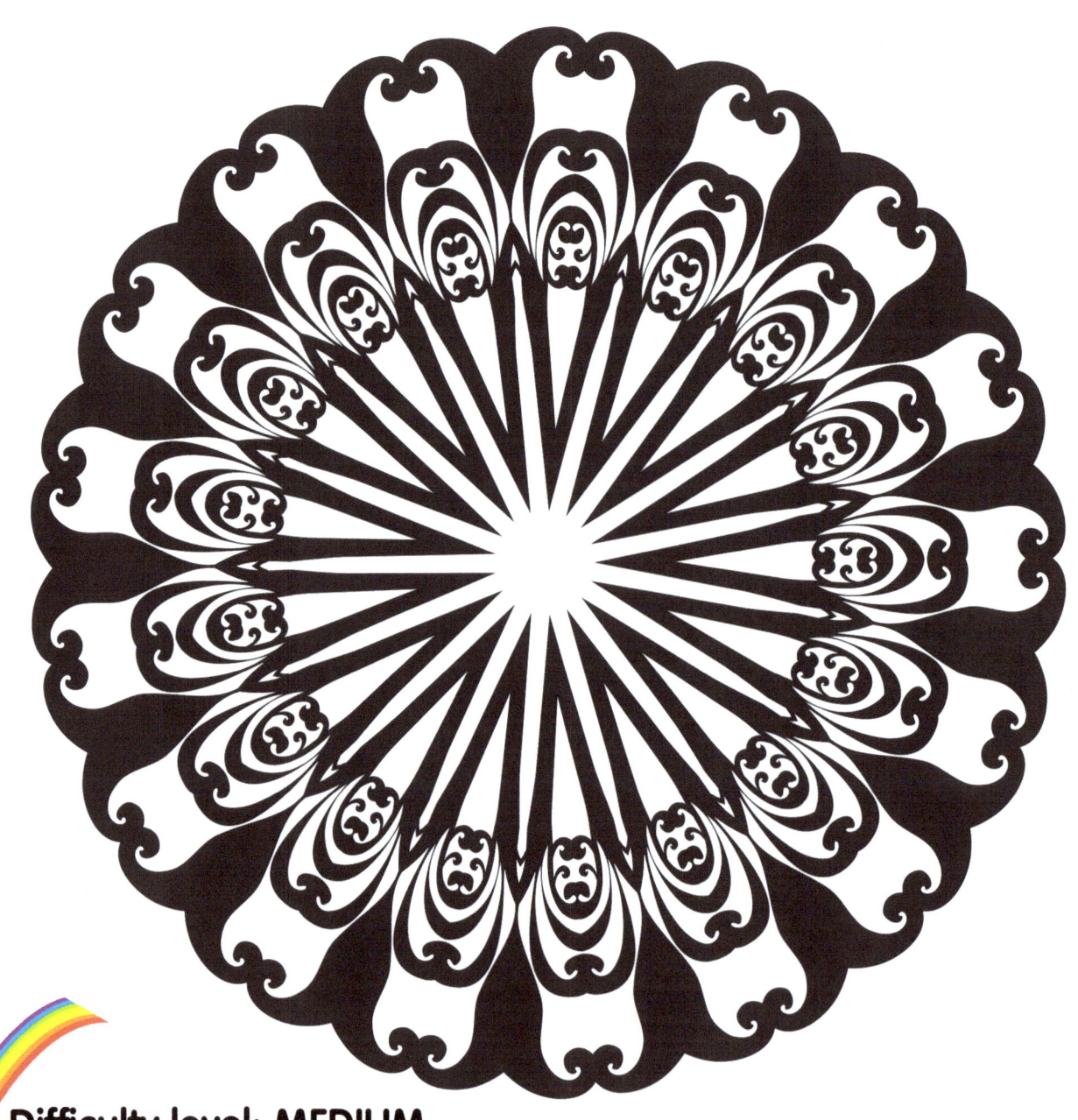

Difficulty level: MEDIUM

DRAWINGS TO COLOR
Creating is Living!

25

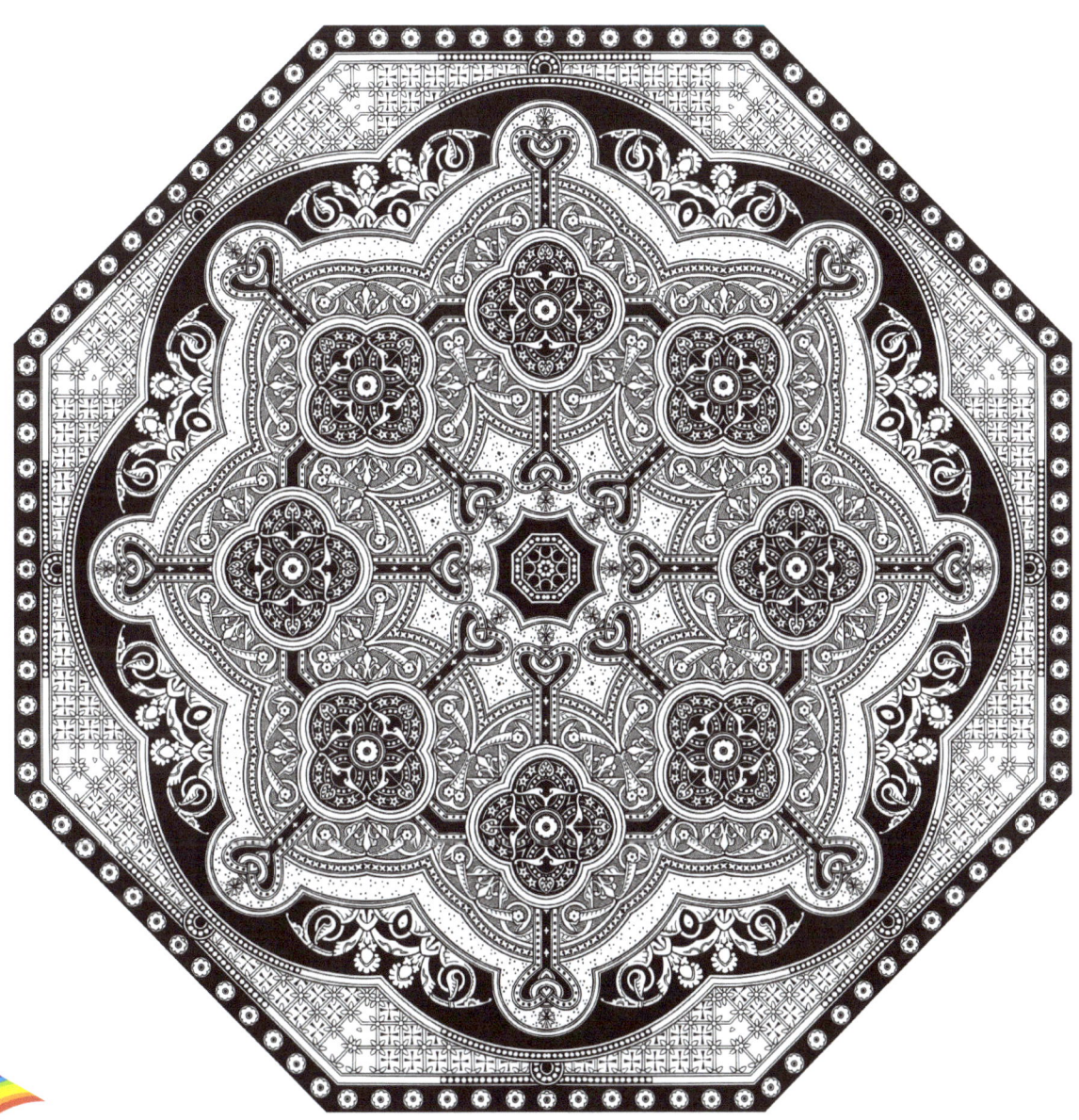

Difficulty level: HARD

26

DRAWINGS TO COLOR
Creating is Living!

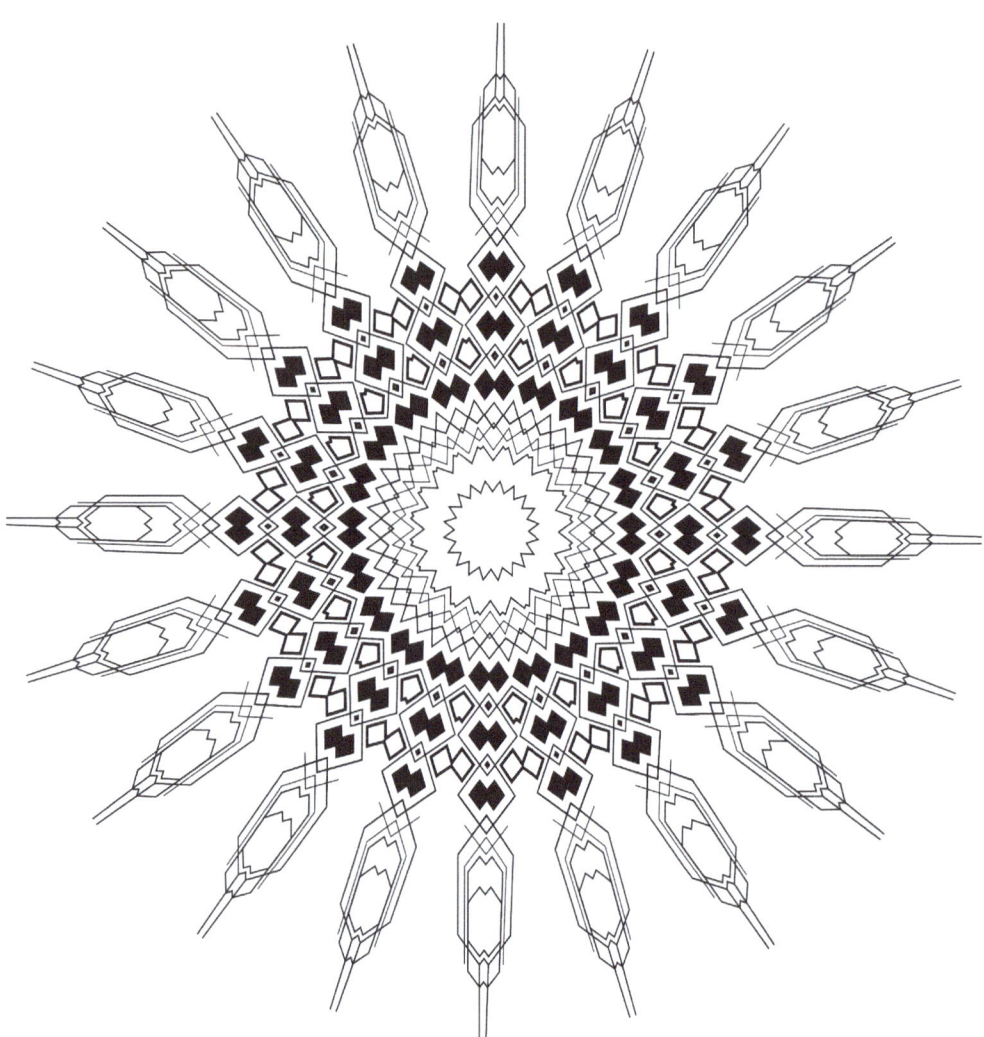

Difficulty level: EASY

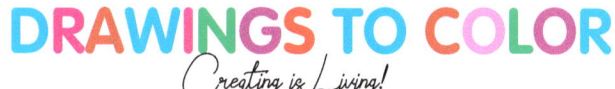

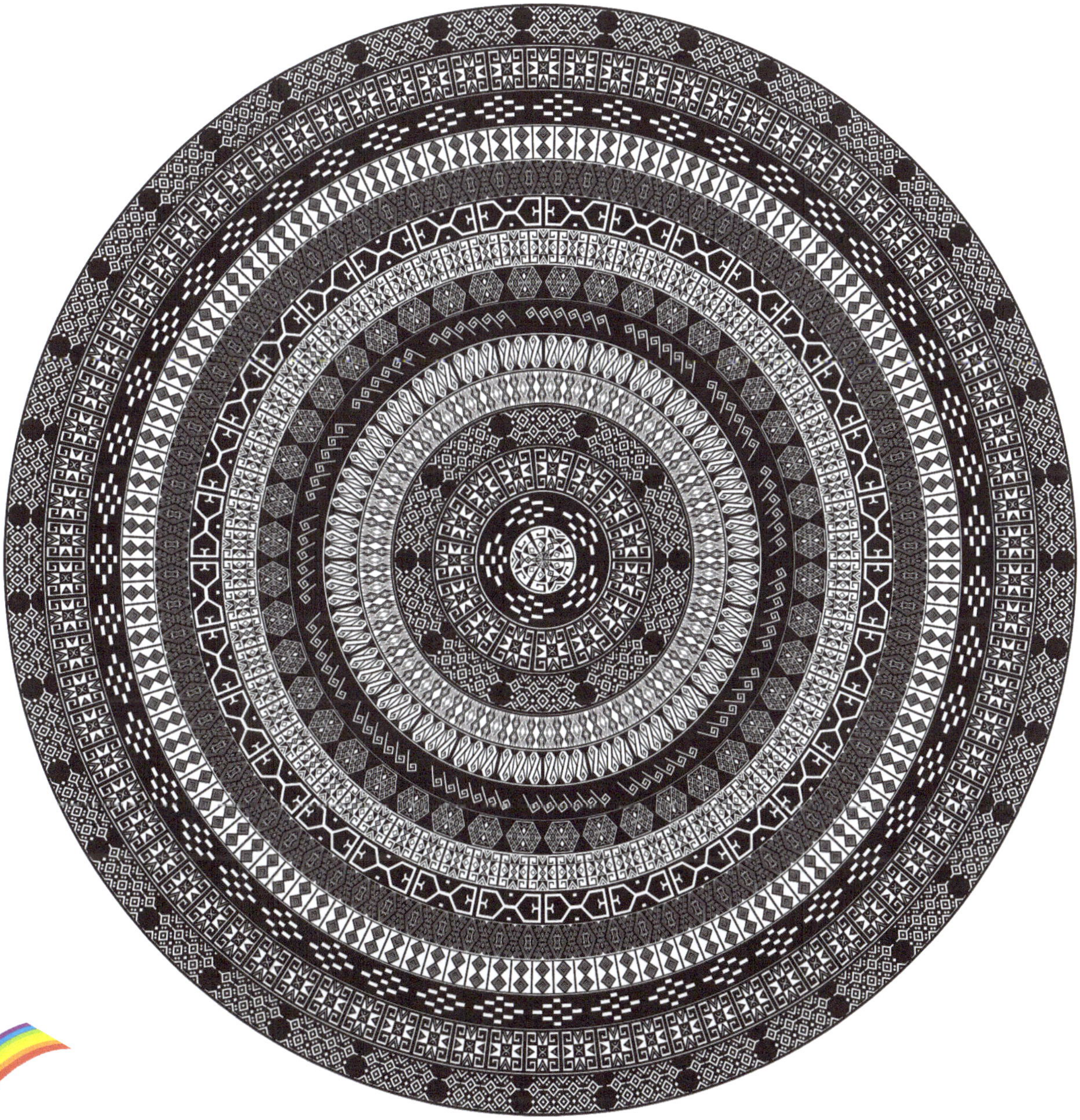

Difficulty level: HARD

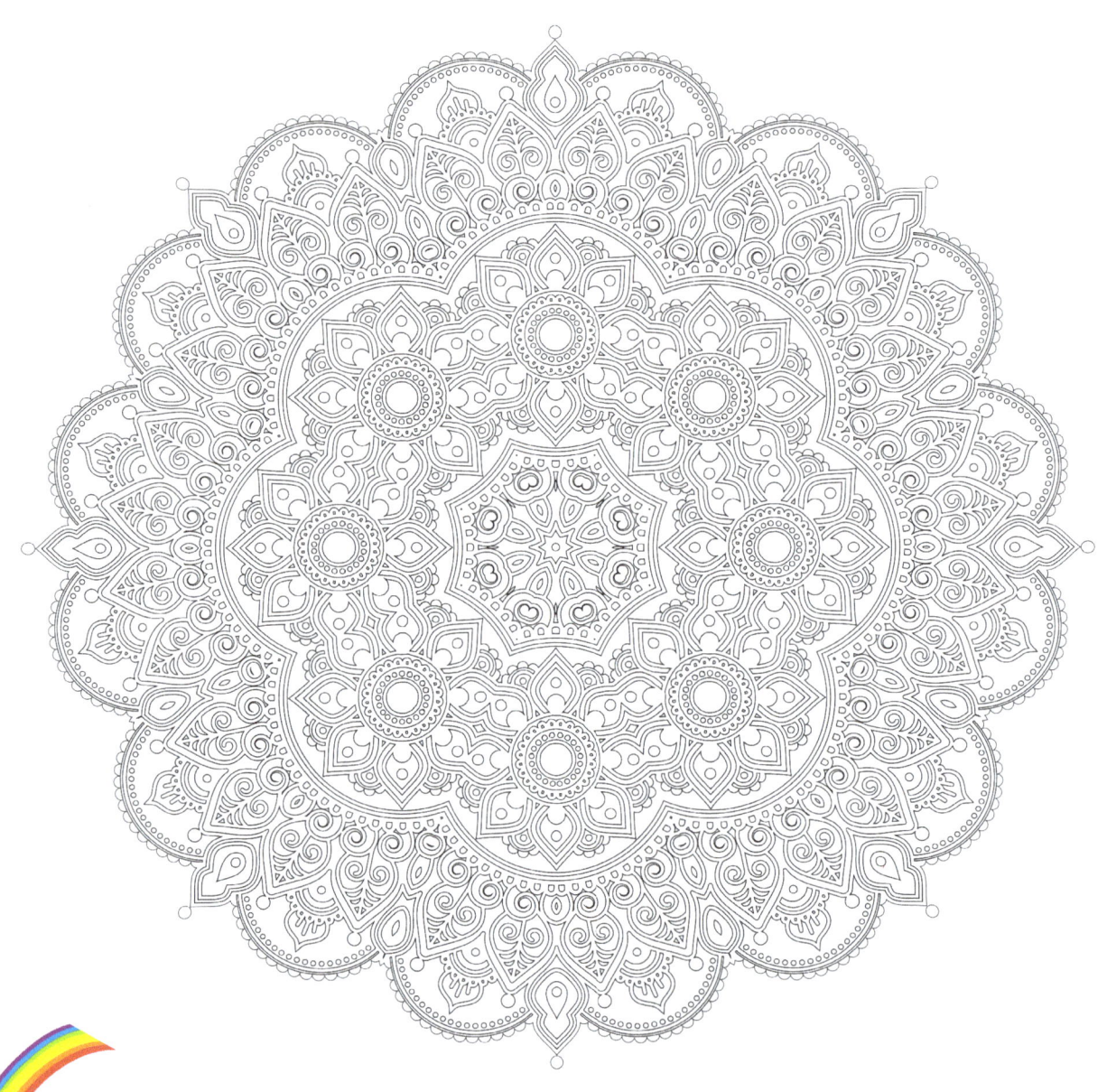

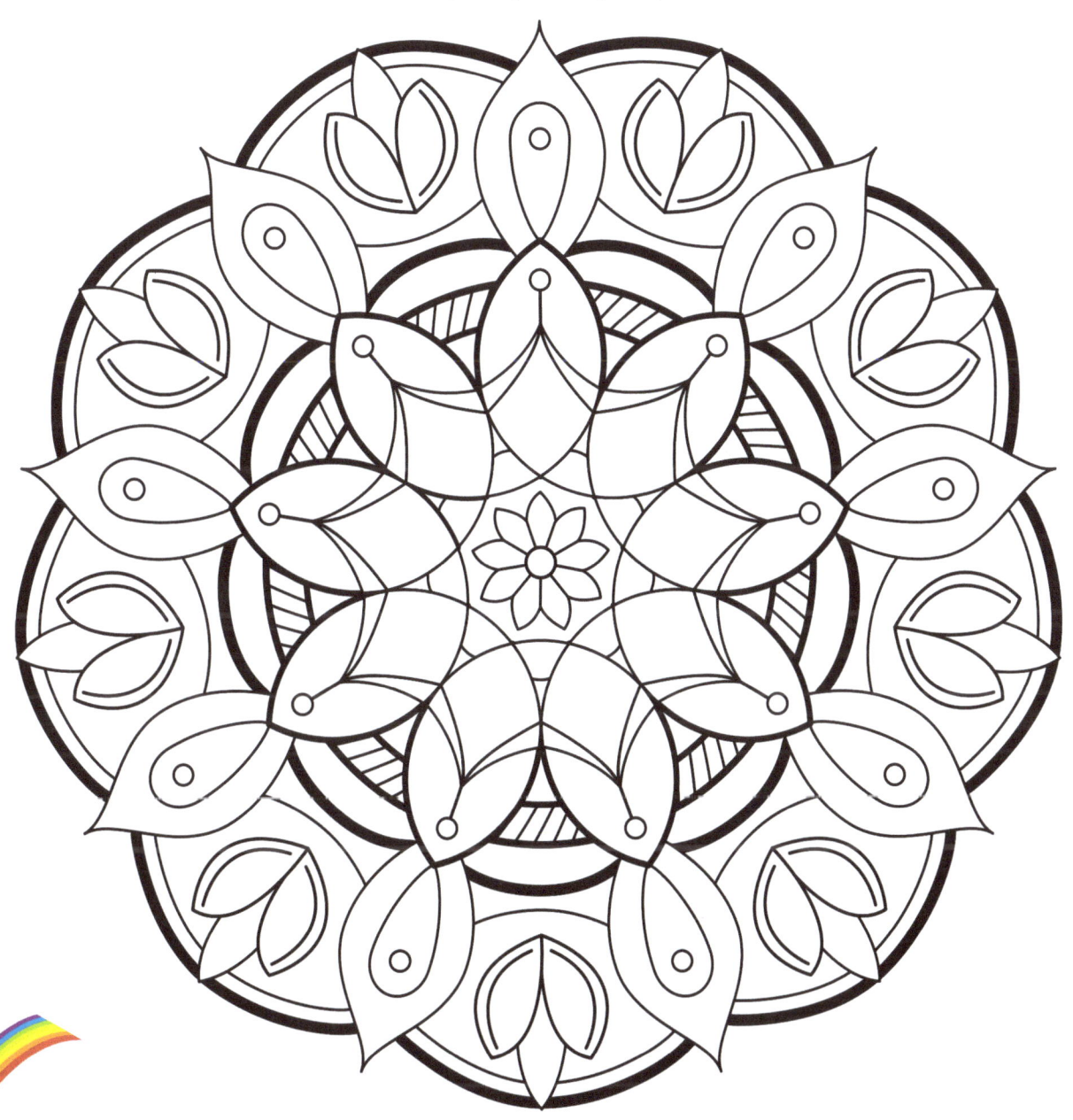

THE

END

What were your experiences?

_____

_____

_____

_____

_____

_____

_____

Show your work!

Photograph the painted drawings and send them to us.

Read the QR Code above, select and attach the photos from the book's pages to the email.

www.ingramcontent.com/pod-product-compliance
Lightning Source LLC
Chambersburg PA
CBHW051821210526
45473CB00005B/1694